SAN FRANCISCO

A PICTURE BOOK TO REMEMBER HER BY

Designed by
DAVID GIBBON

Produced by
TED SMART

Photography by
EDMUND NAGELE

CRESCENT

INTRODUCTION

In the middle of the 18th century, treasure-laden Spanish galleons were a familiar sight along the rugged and often dangerous coast of California. Like many ships before them, they probably failed to notice a narrow inlet which led to a deep, natural harbour known today as San Francisco Bay. It was not until 1775 that a Captain Ayala anchored within the Golden Gate and claimed this part of California for the Spanish Empire.

The following year a mission and a military garrison were established as well as the settlement called Yerba Buena. Spanish control in California, however, did not last long and in 1821 it was taken over by Mexico. This resulted in hostilities breaking out, in the course of which some Americans raised the 'stars and stripes' over the still small but growing outpost of Yerba Buena – which was later to be renamed San Francisco.

What could not possibly have been foreseen at that time was that vast quantities of gold were about to be discovered, firstly in El Dorado county, in the foothills of the Sierra Nevada, in 1848. As a result of this find, eager prospectors from all over the world poured through the Golden Gate and filled the harbour with their ships – many of which were left to rot as their crews joined in the mad scramble for gold.

From the east, more than 42,000 gold prospectors and settlers – the famous 'forty-niners' – travelled to the Great Valley and San Francisco, by way of the California Trail, a hazardous route along which many died.

The growth-rate of San Francisco was extremely rapid and it soon became a riotous place in which to live. Huge fortunes were squandered in the gaming houses and saloons and murder and robbery were rife – committed by those whose contribution to the Gold Rush was to kill and rob some hardworking miner of his gold. One quarter of the town, the Barbary Coast, was deemed to be beyond control because of its violence and lasciviousness. It is said that the town was actually burned and rebuilt six times during these wild days.

When the gold fever finally died down, San Francisco became a virtual ghost town overnight and had to look elsewhere for sources of revenue to bolster its flagging economy. By taking advantage of the region's agricultural produce, and the increasing world trade, the town's situation soon stabilised. Gradually, hills were levelled, streets planned and attractive houses built and San Francisco became, once again, a reputable place in which to live; indeed it was soon the financial and cultural capital of the West.

A second era of excessive spending and rapid development was soon brought about by the discovery of a silver mountain in the nearby state of Nevada in the 1860's. As a consequence even more hotels, theatres, saloons and houses were erected, amongst them lavish, baroque mansions crowning Nob Hill and Russian Hill. These were for the newly rich silver kings, merchants and railroad builders, millionaires whose life-styles astounded poorer folk. The silver bonanza was to have longer-lasting effects on the city than the Gold Rush and for many people San Francisco became the most sophisticated and fashionable city in all America.

Alas, nature – which had so benefited San Francisco – caused, at the peak of the city's development, the greatest disaster in its history. On April 18th, 1906, an earthquake tore apart the very heart of the city. Even worse than the earthquake itself were the extensive fires that followed; fires that were virtually impossible to control due to broken water mains.

San Francisco once again recovered and it is today a cosmopolitan city clinging to the northern tip of a hilly peninsula overlooking the Golden Gate to the north and San Francisco Bay to the east. The sheltered and almost tideless harbour is lined with piers, warehouses and shipyards. As the nearest port to the Far East and Hawaii, San Francisco has important trading links with, particularly, these areas and Australia.

The growth of this great city has been impeded by the rugged nature of the peninsula and most of the recent development has taken place along the shores of the bay, where land is level and relatively cheap. Since 1939 there has been considerable industrial expansion in areas directly related to the products of farming and fishing. The city also continues to be an important commercial and banking centre for a large part of Western America.

For resident and visitor alike, San Francisco is entirely different from any other American city. On the hills are row upon row of distinctive Victorian houses embellished with extravagant turrets and domes, balconies and bay windows, all painted in bright colours. Built mainly of sturdy redwood or fir, these fine houses are an integral part of the San Francisco skyline. So too are the impressive downtown skyscrapers, the tempting restaurants of Fisherman's Wharf and the exclusive shops of Ghirardelli Square, an historic waterfront site and once the home of a renowned chocolate factory.

What was once the site of the tiny village of Yerba Buena is now the exuberant quarter known as Chinatown, and it is here that one of the largest Chinese communities in the western world lives. A maze of narrow streets and alleys evokes the charm and mystery of the East with shops selling exotic goods and countless restaurants serving piquant dishes. Festivals abound, as they do in Japantown, another ethnic neighbourhood. The Japanese love of flowers is reflected in the annual celebration of the Cherry Blossom Festival and in the magnificent floral specimens to be seen in the delightful Tea Garden in Golden Gate Park.

Any description of this wonderful city would be incomplete without mentioning the Cable Cars and the Golden Gate Bridge. The first cable car system was designed by a veteran of the Gold Rush and a wire rope manufacturer named Andrew Hallidie. Prior to this the city's steep hills were traversed by horse-drawn cars which often struggled pathetically when fully laden. In 1880 there were eight lines and the fare was just five cents. Today there are just three lines but the elegant cars are still the most popular way of travelling around the city.

As a symbol of San Francisco, the Golden Gate Bridge is one of the most spectacular sights in the world. Although it is no longer the world's longest single suspension bridge this graceful structure never fails to impress, even when it is partly shrouded in the mists which roll in from the ocean with such frequency. Indeed, the bridge may be said to be an accurate reflection of the strength and beauty of this most unusual city.

Unmistakable in a blue velvet sky is
the Golden Gate Bridge *left* by night.

Silvery Oakland Bay Bridge, with its suspension and cantilever sections both double-decked to accommodate a constant flow of traffic, connects Alameda's capital and seaport of Oakland with San Francisco. Seen *below and below left* from Yerba Buena Island and *left and centre left* from Harrison, the bridge is certainly an engineering masterpiece.

Magnificent by night *top right*, the bridge glows against the twinkling backdrop of a million lights in the skyscrapers beyond, whilst the aerial view *right* of the bridge and Golden Gate with San Francisco is truly awe-inspiring.

As night falls over Oakland Bay Bridge *overleaf* the calm waters deflect the glow from the glittering lights along the shoreline.

San Francisco is the principal port on the Pacific Coast of the U.S.A. and some of its most spectacular views are those taken from the air. *Above left* can be seen the port area, backed by many of the city's modern skyscrapers.

Alcatraz Island, *left, above and centre right* is famous for its long-term Federal Penitentiary, which housed, amongst others, the notorious Al Capone. Although no longer a prison, having been closed in 1962 for economic reasons, it has now become a very unusual tourist attraction and as such attracts countless visitors.

Angle Island *right* is one of the lovely state parks around San Francisco.

Another magnificent night view of Oakland Bridge *overleaf.*

During the last twenty years San Francisco has become an important financial centre and, as a result, soaring skyscrapers *centre and below right* have become a familiar part of the city's landscape, in startling contrast to the old, traditional styles of architecture. In the midst of the modern business section is the gracious, domed City Hall *left*.

One of the most eye-catching buildings is the Transamerica Pyramid *above*, pointing like a needle into the sky and effectively dwarfing the elevations around it.

Many of the skyscrapers afford wonderful views across the San Francisco Bay *left and above right*, showing clearly how the Oakland Bay Bridge connects to Yerba Buena Island and the city of Oakland beyond.

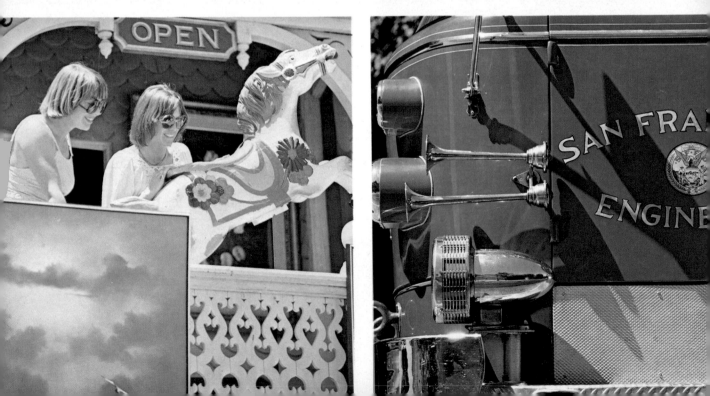

San Francisco is probably the most cosmopolitan city in the world. American, Oriental and European influences are seen everywhere, in the buildings, shops, restaurants, and the people themselves.

The Oakland Bay Bridge *overleaf* merges into the city of San Francisco.

The aerial photograph *top left* shows one of the busy freeway intersections twisting and coiling through the city.

Wending its way through wooded parkland, and the dazzling blue bay beyond, is Highway 101 *centre left*.

Across the Golden Gate Bridge is the charming town of Sausalito *below left*, a favourite retreat for city dwellers and enthusiastic yachtsmen.

The roof-top view *above right* shows houses of an earlier era, gaily painted and reflecting several styles of architecture, all jostling for space in this tightly packed region.

The semi-circular Palace of Fine Arts dominates the scene in this aerial view *right*. It was constructed in 1915 for the Panama-Pacific International Exposition, by the architect Bernard Maybeck.

Stanford University *left* lies in the
centre of the campus and was built in
1883 of native sandstone, by Leland
Stanford. Its beautiful memorial church,
whose sublime interior can be seen
below, was dedicated to the Senator by
his wife, shortly after his death in 1893.
The superb Venetian mosaics gracing
the exterior are shown *below centre*,
whilst several examples of the exquisite
stained glass windows can be viewed
right.

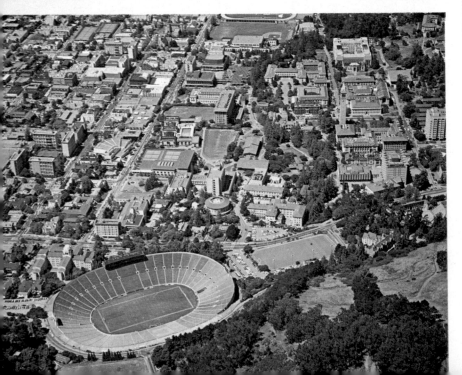

Berkeley, whose university is the oldest
of all California's nine campuses,
stands on San Francisco Bay and can be
seen *left* in this magnificent aerial view.
It is particularly famous for its atomic
research programme and visitors are
welcome to the demonstrations held in
the complex.

Another breathtaking view of Oakland
Bay Bridge *overleaf*, set against the
silver ripples in the Bay.

San Francisco's geographical position, together with its development as the largest seaport on the West Coast, led to its importance as the "Gateway to the Orient". This resulted in the largest Chinese community living outside the Orient being massed together in what is known as "Chinatown".

These are typical and colourful street scenes *above left and below far left*, where even the street signs are bilingual *above right*. Many shops sell precious jade and ivory objects *near left* and exquisite silk embroideries and porcelain *right*.

Grant Avenue by night *overleaf* shows the clamour of this noted street which extends from north to south through Chinatown.

Although a poor imitation of the original Barbary Coast which emerged in the days of the "Gold Rush" in California, Broadway, with its blazing lights, bars, clubs and restaurants, *above, far left and right*, still attracts many visitors, whilst the exotic dancer *near left* can be seen at the El Cid Club.

Car headlamps compete with the garish and provocative signs outside Broadway's buildings *overleaf*.

The fine Victorian and Edwardian houses shown on this page are part of San Francisco's tradition. Many are brightly painted and well kept but others, alas, are falling into disrepair, giving way to modern, more easily maintained apartment blocks.

The narrow Fresnol Street with its weatherboard houses can be seen *overleaf right* and the colourful and imaginative murals by Mujeres Muralistas *left* make a decorative addition to Mission St.

One of the most picturesque streets in San Francisco is Lombard *above and left,* which winds tortuously downhill between Leavenworth and Hyde, affording magnificent views to drivers and pedestrians alike. By contrast the almost vertical Fresnol St. *right* rises precipitously and on the brow can be seen one of the city's famous cable cars.

California St. *overleaf left,* looking out over the Oakland Bay Bridge, parodies San Francisco's love for development and tradition alike.

Powell St. ascending to the historic Nob Hill area, can be seen *overleaf right.*

The popular cable cars *above* in Hyde St. and *left* in California St. are a novel yet highly efficient method of travelling in this hilly city. A cable car crosses Powell St. *right*; the impressive Transamerica Pyramid dominating the scene.

In the heart of the city is Union Square *overleaf*, seen from the luxurious St. Francis Hotel.

The geometric Justin Herman Plaza is shown *left,* its stepping stones pacing through the Fountain Pool.

Embarcadero Plaza, in the financial district *centre left,* contains the controversial fountain, holding 101 concrete boxes, which was designed by Armand Vaillancourt and is in direct contrast to the architecture of the City Hall *below left.*

Hallidie Plaza and Market St. *above,* with its sunken plaza also contains the Visitors' Information Center.

San Francisco has many superb hotels, including the Hyatt Regency with its tree and flower-filled lobby, *pictured right.*

A wonderful panoramic view of the city *overleaf* seen from Twin Peaks.

The Transamerica Pyramid standing 853 ft. high on the skyline is seen from Montgomery St. *above,* from Edith Coolbrith Park *centre right* and from Columbus *below right.*

Above right the illuminated skyscrapers glow in the background on Steiner St., whilst *left* are two general views of the city.

The corner of Columbus and Pacific St. can be seen *below* and *overleaf* San Francisco by night from Edith Coolbrith Park.

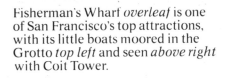

Fisherman's Wharf *overleaf* is one of San Francisco's top attractions, with its little boats moored in the Grotto *top left* and seen *above right* with Coit Tower.

The Cannery *centre left* with its many restaurants is a multi-million dollar development of this old Victorian landmark; of particular note is Ghirardelli Square, features of which can be seen *above and below*.

The Balclutha *below left*, the last ship to round Cape Horn bringing immigrants to California, is moored in the Wharf's vicinity, whilst *below right* is Russian Hill.

Six lanes of traffic noisily cross the famous Golden Gate Bridge *left*, the bridge they said could never be built, whilst *below* the impressive bronze statue commemorates the builder of the bridge, Joseph Strauss, whose engineering masterpiece spans 4,200 feet across the bay.

Standing under the south tower of the bridge, historic Fort Point *below* was built in the mid-19th century to guard the Golden Gate. Although 127 cannon were mounted they were never needed and today the site is preserved as a national monument.

Two more magnificent views of the bridge *right*, seen on a clear day; however, this is rare, for as shown *overleaf* the rolling fog often thickly envelopes the bridge, blotting out most of the view.

San Francisco and Oakland can be seen in the background as the Golden Gate Bridge spans the bay *above left*.

Another aspect *left*; this time lovely Sausalito with its steep hillside seen behind the bridge.

Below right is shown a section of the Golden Gate, the world's largest and tallest single span suspension bridge which was completed in 1937 at a cost of over 35 million dollars.

Unforgettable by night, sunset floods the bridge *above right*.

For those brave enough to try, surfing under the bridge *left* is an exciting experience.

The Golden Gate Park is both beautiful and exotic, extending to over 1,000 acres. The Japanese Tea Gardens *above* and Buddha statue *below* are exquisite examples of oriental art.

The much visited Victorian Conservatory *above right* with its outstanding collection of flora can be seen *centre right* from the interior, whilst *below right* the elegant dolphins swim in the Steinhart Aquarium.

Muir Woods, Marin County *overleaf*, contains many magnificent redwood trees.

First published in Great Britain 1978 by Colour Library International Ltd.
© Illustrations: Colour Library International Ltd. Colour separations by La Cromolito, Milan, Italy.
Display and text filmsetting by Focus Photoset, London, England.
Printed by I.G. Domingo and bound by Eurobinder, Barcelona (Spain)
Published by Crescent Books, a division of Crown Publishers Inc.
Library of Congress Catalogue Card No. 78-60221
CRESCENT 1984